001.94 OXL

This book is to be returned on or before
the last date sta    be

11. OCT 07

# The Mystery
## of the
# Bermuda Triangle

**Chris Oxlade**

**Heinemann**
**LIBRARY**

First published in Great Britain by Heinemann Library,
Halley Court, Jordan Hill, Oxford OX2 8EJ,
a division of Reed Educational and Professional Publishing Ltd.
Heinemann is a registered trademark of Reed Educational & Professional
Publishing Limited.

OXFORD  MELBOURNE  AUCKLAND
JOHANNESBURG  BLANTYRE  GABORONE
IBADAN  PORTSMOUTH NH (USA)  CHICAGO

Designed by **AMR** Ltd, Bramley, Hants, England
Illustrations by Art Construction and Margaret Payne at AMR
Printed in Hong Kong

03 02 01 00
10 9 8 7 6 5 4 3 2

ISBN 0 431 01631 3

**British Library Cataloguing in Publication Data**

Oxlade, Chris
  Bermuda Triangle. – (Can science solve?)
  1.Science – Methodology – Juvenile literature 2.Bermuda
  Triangle – Juvenile literature
  I.Title II.Wallace, Holly
  001.94

  ISBN 0 431 01631 3

**Acknowledgements**

The Publishers would like to thank the following for permission to reproduce
photographs: Austin J Brown: pp11, 13, 15; James Davis Travel Photography: p28;
Mary Evans Picture Library: pp5, 6, 9; Eye Ubiquitous: p16, S Lindridge p22; FLPA:
D Fleetham/Silvestris p7 (inset), H Hoflinger p17, D Kinzler p18; Fortean Picture
Library: pp24, 27, W Donato p21; National Archives: pp8, 10; The People: p29;
Trip: E Smith p7 (main).

Cover photograph reproduced with permission of H Hoflinger, FLPA.

Every effort has been made to contact copyright holders of any material
reproduced in this book. Any omissions will be rectified in subsequent printings
if notice is given to the Publisher.

Any words appearing in bold, **like this**, are explained in the Glossary.

# Contents

# Unsolved mysteries

For centuries, people have been puzzled and fascinated by mysterious places, creatures and events. What secrets does a black hole hold? Are some houses really haunted by ghosts? Does the Abominable Snowman actually exist? Why do ships and planes vanish without trace when they cross the Bermuda Triangle? These mysteries have baffled scientists, who have spent years trying to find the answers. But just how far can science go? Can it really explain the seemingly unexplainable? Or are there some mysteries which science simply cannot solve? Read on, and make your own mind up....

This book tells you about the Bermuda Triangle. It looks in detail at some of the unexplained disappearances that have happened in it, retells accounts from eyewitnesses and investigates whether science can account for some of these bizarre events.

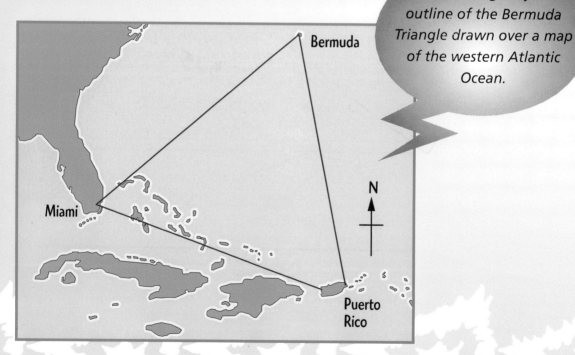

The imaginary outline of the Bermuda Triangle drawn over a map of the western Atlantic Ocean.

# Bermuda Triangle briefing

Bermuda is made up of about 150 small islands, 1000 kilometres out into the Atlantic Ocean from the eastern coast of the USA. The area known as the Bermuda Triangle is, not surprisingly, a triangle with its three points in Bermuda, Miami and Puerto Rico (see map). The term Bermuda Triangle was first used by American journalist Vincent Gaddis in 1964 when he wrote a magazine article with the title 'The Deadly Bermuda Triangle', in which he listed mysterious disappearances in the area.

Over the last 200 years, thousands of boats, ships and aircraft have come to grief in the Bermuda Triangle. Most of these cases have a perfectly reasonable explanation, but almost a hundred of them remain a mystery. Could they be caused by some strange, unknown force? Is there anything science can do to solve the mystery?

*Disappearances in the Bermuda Triangle gave rise to many wild and wonderful stories in science-fiction magazines.*

JUNE
25 CENTS
IN CANADA 30 CENTS

# AMAZING STORIES

Scientifiction
Stories by

A. Hyatt Verrill
John W. Campbell, Jr.
Edmond Hamilton

## Triangle or trapezium?

*Many writers do not agree about the boundaries of the Bermuda Triangle. A few say that it is a triangle, others that it is an elongated, four-sided shape called the 'Devil's Triangle' or the 'Limbo of the Lost', which stretches further into the Atlantic.*

# Beginnings of a mystery

Although it was not until the 1960s that the Bermuda Triangle became famous, it had been an area of mystery for sailors long before then. It all started when early transatlantic voyagers, including Christopher Columbus, who first sailed through the Bermuda Triangle area in 1492, encountered unfamiliar sights and strange goings-on.

*Christopher Columbus sailed through the Triangle in the* Santa Maria, *a small ship called a caravel.*

## A sea of weed

One of these strange sights was the area now known as the Sargasso Sea, an oval-shaped patch of the North Atlantic several thousand kilometres across, stretching well into the Bermuda Triangle. In the Sargasso Sea, the water is normally calm, with little wind and **current**, and the water is also more salty than the surrounding sea, with very little **plankton** and very few fish. Strangest of all, there are great rafts of seaweed called Sargassum weed. Seaweed is hardly ever found in the open ocean.

*Calm waters in the Sargasso Sea. The inset shows drifting Sargassum weed being eaten by a Sargassum fish.*

To the early sailors, the seaweed suggested that they were near land, so they were confused when no land appeared. The weed also became tangled with their ships, slowing them down, and the light winds often left them drifting for days on end. It's no wonder, then, that tales spread of ships trapped forever or pulled under the sea by the weeds and of sailors eaten by hideous sea creatures.

Columbus also reported seeing strange lights in the sky in the area, and the fact that his ships' compasses behaved strangely. And when, ten years after his first trip, he returned with a fleet of ships, he lost twelve in a fierce **hurricane**. The island of Bermuda itself was not settled until about a hundred years later than this, mainly because it had a reputation as a 'place for devils'.

There is no doubt that hundreds of ships were lost in the Bermuda Triangle over the following centuries. Many sank without trace and were assumed to have been overwhelmed by storms. The first ship that is mentioned in the literature on the Bermuda Triangle is the American warship USS *Pickering*, which disappeared without trace in 1800.

# Ships and boats

Losses of ships and boats in the Bermuda Triangle fall in two groups – those where the ship or boat disappeared without trace and those where the ship or boat was found with the crew missing.

## Spray

(**sloop**, vanished in 1909)
The *Spray* was sailed by Joshua Slocum, an experienced sailor who was the first man to sail single-handed around the world. It disappeared with Slocum, who was 65 years old at the time, after he had visited Miami for supplies.

*The disappearance of the USS* Cyclops *was described as 'one of the most baffling mysteries in the annals of the Navy'.*

## Cyclops

(US Navy **collier**, vanished in 1918)
The *Cyclops*, 165 metres long, weighing 17,500 tonnes and with 300 crew, is one of the largest ships lost in the Triangle. It was carrying ore and disappeared without trace *en route* from Barbados to the eastern United States. The *Cyclops* was the first ship to disappear which carried a radio, but the crew sent no emergency message.

# Carroll A Deering

(five-masted **schooner**, found abandoned in 1921)
The *Carroll A Deering* left Rio de Janeiro without cargo to return to Norfolk, Virginia. Several weeks later it was seen by the crew of a **lightship**, under full sail with the crew all together on the deck. One of the crew shouted that they had lost both anchors. Two days later the ship was found beached on the shore with the sails still set and the lifeboats and crew's belongings on board. But the crew themselves were missing, and were never seen again.

# Marine Sulphur Queen

(cargo-ship, vanished in 1963)
The *Marine Sulphur Queen* left Texas carrying a cargo of molten sulphur. A search was started when it could not be contacted after failing to send a routine radio message. Some debris, including a foghorn and life-jacket, was found.

# The *Mary Celeste*

*Easily the most famous mystery of the sea is the case of the* Mary Celeste, *a small sail-powered cargo-ship which was found drifting without its crew in 1872. The case of the* Mary Celeste *is often linked with the Bermuda Triangle, but it was actually found near the Azores, which are nearer Spain than America. According to many accounts of the case, the ship appeared as normal, with all the crew's possessions and all the cargo on board. It seemed that the crew had magically vanished. However, there was some damage to the rigging, the lifeboat was missing and the hold was full of sea water. The most likely explanation of the many put forward is that the crew were convinced that the ship was about to sink and abandoned it in a hurry without taking down the sails. The ship continued to sail, leaving them behind in mid ocean in an overloaded boat.*

# Into thin air

In all these cases of aircraft which have disappeared in the Bermuda Triangle, not a scrap of the aircraft or any sign of survivors was ever found.

## Flight 19

(five US Navy bombers and a rescue plane, vanished in 1945) The case of Flight 19 is the most famous of all. It is mysterious because a group of five aircraft vanished at the same time, along with the search plane that was sent to find them, which seems a very unlikely event. There are many different accounts of this case, but here are the basic facts.

*A Martin Mariner seaplane, similar to the one that was sent to search for Flight 19.*

At 2 pm on 5 December, five Avenger torpedo bombers took off in good weather from Fort Lauderdale, Florida on a routine training mission which should have lasted two hours. The first signs of trouble appeared at 3.45 pm, when the pilots realized they were lost. The flight leader, Lieutenant Taylor, reported that both his compasses were 'out'. A flight instructor from Fort Lauderdale offered to fly south to meet them, but Taylor replied 'I know where I am now. Don't come after me.'

Messages between the planes were heard at about 7 pm, and a Martin Mariner seaplane was sent to search for them at 7.30 pm. Nothing more was heard from any of the Avengers or the Mariner, and an extensive air-sea rescue search found no sign of the 27 airmen.

## Star Tiger

(Tudor IV airliner, vanished in 1948)
After flying from the Azores, the British airliner *Star Tiger* had nearly reached Bermuda when the pilot radioed that the weather was good and that he expected to arrive on time. But the aircraft never arrived, and a search for survivors and wreckage revealed nothing.

## Douglas DC-3

(airliner, vanished in 1948)
This aircraft was flying to Miami, Florida from Puerto Rico. The pilot reported by radio that he was 80 kilometres south of the airfield, but soon after this the airfield could not get a response from the DC-3. A search found no sign of the aircraft, even though the water in the area where it disappeared was only six metres deep. The DC-3 had simply vanished.

*An Avro Tudor airliner similar to the one that disappeared over the Triangle in 1948.*

# Did you see that?

Many people have had strange experiences as they travelled through the Bermuda Triangle, but lived to tell the tale. Here are the stories of a few of them.

## Crew of Boeing 707

Soon after take-off from San Juan in 1963, the crew of a 707 saw the sea below them froth up for about 30 seconds. The disturbed area was about a kilometre across and the froth reached several hundred metres into the air.

## Chuck Wakely

In 1964, Wakely was flying from Nassau in the Bahamas to Miami. He noticed a faint glow on the wings, which gradually increased to a blinding light. At the same time, the aircraft's electrical equipment began to go wrong. After five minutes, the glow gradually faded and things returned to normal.

## Captain Don Henry

Henry was the captain of a **salvage tug**. In 1966 it was towing a barge when it experienced electrical and engine failures and the compass started spinning out-of-control. Henry went out on deck to find the horizon obscured by fog, the sea choppy and the barge invisible, even though the tow rope was still tight. After a while the engines began working again and the tug moved forwards. As it did, the barge reappeared and was found to be warm to the touch.

# Bruce Gernon

In 1970, Gernon was flying a small private aircraft through the Triangle when he flew into a 'strange cloud'. While in the cloud, his instruments and compass failed and he felt weightless for a few seconds. When he landed, he realized that he had taken half an hour less than he thought was possible for the flight.

# Crew of the USS *Richard E Byrd*

In 1971, this naval destroyer lost the use of all its communications equipment *en route* to Bermuda. The ship was lost and helpless at sea for more than a week before its radio began to work again.

*Many of the stories of strange happenings in the Bermuda Triangle involve **navigational** instruments. Could this be the key to solving the mystery?*

# Crew of the *Hollyhock*

In 1974, the **radar** aboard the *Hollyhock*, a US Coast Guard boat, detected a large land mass, like an island, in the ocean. The radar was checked, but seemed to be working properly. Other ships also reported the same event. As the boat travelled towards it, the object disappeared.

# The theories

What are the possible explanations for the strange cases listed on the previous pages? A look at the reasons for marine and air accidents all over the world shows that there is a wide range of possible reasons for every disappearance in the Bermuda Triangle.

The first thing to note is that if you compare the number of accidents and disappearances in the Bermuda Triangle to the number of ships and aircraft passing through it, the Bermuda Triangle does not seem to be a particularly dangerous place. In fact, Lloyd's, the world's shipping insurer, says that there are no more losses than in any other shipping area.

## A simple explanation

Most losses at sea and in the air are not in the slightest bit mysterious – and that includes losses in the Bermuda Triangle. They are caused by mechanical failure, bad weather, human error or a combination of the three.

There are several ways a ship can be sunk. Its **hull** can be holed by hitting an object in or under the water, which allows water in from underneath; it can be damaged in a collision; it can simply break apart; or it can capsize because it is top heavy, overloaded or its cargo moves to one side. Obviously, bad weather makes all these events more likely. In the case of a collision, a smaller craft can be hit and sunk by a much larger craft without the crew of the larger craft even noticing, especially at night.

In an aircraft, a structural failure, such as the loss of a wing, or a control failure, such as the **rudder** jamming, can bring it down very quickly. In both ships and aircraft, there can also be fires or explosions because of dangerous cargo or leaking fuel tanks.

## Human factors

Mistakes by ships' crews and aircraft pilots can cause accidents. At sea, where there are no landmarks, **navigational** errors can lead to ships and aircraft without modern navigational equipment becoming hopelessly lost. This is almost certainly what happened to the ill-fated Flight 19 – the aircraft probably ran out of fuel and crashed into the ocean. Bad design or poor maintenance can also be responsible for mechanical failures. A few ships also disappear without trace because of **insurance** fraud, **sabotage** and the actions of modern-day pirates.

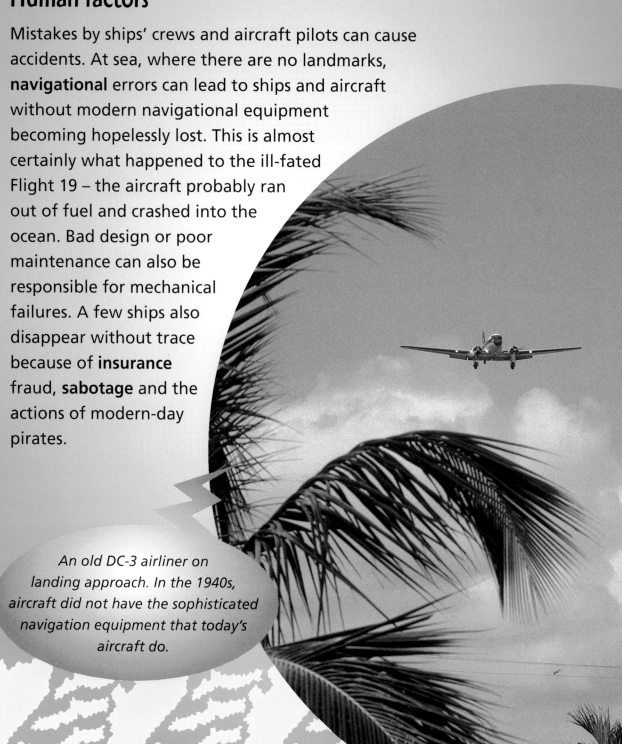

*An old DC-3 airliner on landing approach. In the 1940s, aircraft did not have the sophisticated navigation equipment that today's aircraft do.*

# Strange weather

The seas in the Bermuda Triangle are often featured in holiday brochures, where they look calm, turquoise and shallow. But in fact, the area is prone to very bad storms, from squally thunderstorms to **tornadoes** and **hurricanes**. The storms are often more sudden and violent than anywhere else in the world. So does the weather hold the answer to some of the mysterious disappearances?

## Hurricanes and storms

Hurricanes are enormous, swirling weather systems which are born in the Atlantic near the Equator and sweep north, normally into the Caribbean Sea and the Gulf of Mexico. In the centre of a hurricane, winds can reach average speeds of more than 150 kilometres per hour, gusting to 300 kilometres per hour.

Thunderstorms are created when warm, damp air rises into the atmosphere and **condenses**. They can be huge and severe in the Bermuda Triangle, with clouds reaching up to 15,000 metres high and measuring several kilometres across. Under the clouds are strong, gusty winds and sometimes small, hurricane-like mini storms called neitercanes.

*A hurricane photographed from space. The strongest winds are near the centre of the swirl of cloud.*

16

These super-strong hurricane and storm winds, and the huge waves they create, can overwhelm and capsize small boats, cause ships to break apart and blow them off course. Inside the storm clouds themselves, the winds are very turbulent – they blow up and down as well as sideways. Aircraft flying through them are tossed about, occasionally so fiercely that their structure is damaged.

A waterspout is a tornado that sucks up water from the sea, destroying any small craft in its way.

## Freak waves

Even large ships have been capsized by individual **freak waves**, which can be up to 35 metres high. They may be caused by undersea earthquakes or volcanic eruptions, landslides on the **continental shelf** or by storm waves building together.

## Currents

The water in the Bermuda Triangle also has strong **currents** flowing in it. These include the strong, north-flowing current called the Gulf Stream, which flows at about seven kilometres per hour. Wind blowing in the opposite direction to the current can create very steep waves which can swamp and capsize small craft. These currents could explain many of the unsuccessful air-sea searches in the Bermuda Triangle because by the time the rescue services arrive at the scene of the accident, the wreckage would have been swept away and dispersed.

# Electricity and magnetism

Many travellers in the Bermuda Triangle experience strange magnetic and electrical effects, such as spinning compasses, failed electrical equipment, drained batteries, radio interference and peculiar lights. Are there any natural **phenomena** that could explain these effects?

## Lightning

The heat created by a lightning strike can cause explosions on ships and in aircraft if the sparks ignite fuel or fuel vapour inside empty fuel tanks, and can sink wooden ships by punching holes in the hull. The huge **electric currents** in lightning also create strong **magnetic fields** which can make compasses swing and interfere with radio communications.

*Lightning happens when static electricity which builds up inside a cloud jumps to the ground.*

## Ball lightning

Ball lightning is very rare and not fully understood by scientists, but it could explain some of the strange lights seen in the Triangle. It comes in the form of a ball of coloured light, normally about 25 centimetres across, and forms in **electrical storms**. The ball can hover and move about, as if under remote control.

# Strange magnetic fields

The Earth acts as a giant magnet, with its **magnetic poles** near, but not in the same place as, its **geographic poles**. A magnetic compass points towards magnetic north, which is the direction towards the magnetic North Pole. In most places on the Earth's surface, there is a difference between magnetic north and true north. But the Bermuda Triangle is on a line through both the geographic North Pole and the magnetic North Pole, so the two directions are the same. A compass pointing to true north seems strange to sailors and pilots from other areas of the world, and it could explain some **navigational** errors in the Triangle.

Another confusing compass error, which happens in many areas of the world, including some parts of the Bermuda Triangle, is when the compass turns away from magnetic north. These incidents are often caused by hidden deposits of iron ore or magnetic rocks under the ground, which distort the Earth's magnetic field. The effect is called a **magnetic anomaly**. Temporary magnetic anomalies could also be caused by **magma** flowing near the Earth's surface, undersea earthquakes and electrical storms. It is possible that these events could set up extremely strong magnetic fields, which could affect electrical equipment as well as compasses.

*A piece of iron changes the shape of a magnet's field just as magnetic rocks affect the Earth's magnetic field.*

magnetic field

magnet

magnetic field

iron lump

magnet

Bar magnet with field

Iron lump distorts field

# Weird and wonderful

Several Bermuda Triangle 'experts' who have written books on the subject claim that the strange events that happen there cannot have natural explanations. How, they say, can huge ships and whole groups of aircraft simply disappear in calm weather and shallow seas? Instead, they argue that some sort of supernatural forces are involved. The only evidence for these theories is the lack of evidence – that the disappeared craft and people have never been found.

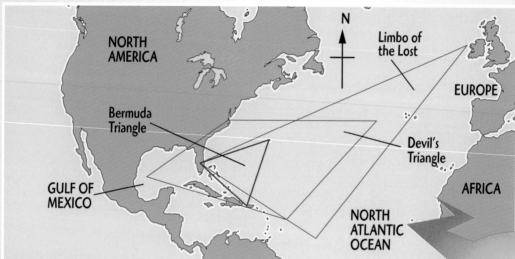

## Vile vortices

Ivan T Sanderson drew up a map of areas where strange disappearances happen, including the Bermuda Triangle and the 'Devil's Sea' near Japan. He suggests that there are twelve such areas, which he calls 'vile **vortices**', where there are massive **magnetic anomalies** which create time slips and mysteriously transport objects to other places on Earth. However, there does not seem to be any statistical evidence to support this.

*Writers dispute the boundaries of the Bermuda Triangle, possibly so that disappearances can be included in their arguments.*

# Aliens and Atlantis

One of the most popular theories for the Bermuda Triangle disappearances is that the ships and aircraft, or the people on them, have been abducted by aliens and carried away for investigation and experimentation. Ivan T Sanderson claims that there could be an advanced civilization under the ocean below the Bermuda Triangle, and that the ships and aircraft are taken there.

*Underwater ruins near the island of Bimini, claimed to be the remains of Atlantis.*

The most famous Bermuda Triangle writer, Charles Berlitz, has suggested that Atlantis, the legendary lost land, was near the island of Bimini in the Bahamas, on the western edge of the Bermuda Triangle. The technology of Atlantis remains there and is automatically sinking ships and shooting down aircraft. The legend of Atlantis comes from writings of the Greek philosopher Plato. There is no proof that it ever existed.

# Black holes

Vincent Gaddis, the man who coined the phrase 'Bermuda Triangle' in 1964, suggested in the same article that ships and planes may be disappearing through a 'gateway' (possibly a mini **black hole**) into another time or another universe. This could explain why some aircraft travelling through the Bermuda Triangle arrive at their destination more quickly than should have been possible, although **navigational** errors and unexpected strong winds are a more likely explanation.

# A modern theory

In 1995, an international organization called the Ocean Drilling Programme began to investigate the ocean floor between Bermuda and the coast of the United States. They were looking for **methane** escaping from the rocks under the ocean floor, which could possibly be used as an energy source. What has this got to do with the Bermuda Triangle? The huge bubbles of methane escaping from the ocean bed could rise to the surface, affecting ships and aircraft above.

## Gas hydrates

The strange thing about the methane gas the drillers found was that it was in the form of gas hydrate. This means that it was mixed with frozen water. In methane hydrate, the methane is locked up inside the ice. Methane hydrate is formed when a mixture of water and methane is squeezed by very high pressure deep under the sea bed. When the pressure is released or the temperature rises, the methane is released. When just one litre of icy hydrate melts, it releases 170 litres of methane.

*Methane released from the ocean floor could explain some accidents on oil and gas drilling rigs.*

Scientists think that there is a huge amount of methane hydrate under the oceans, formed as dead animals and plants **decompose** in the **sediments** on the ocean floor. In fact, methane hydrates have been found under the ocean in the Bermuda Triangle.

# Bubble trouble

Imagine what would happen if a deposit of methane hydrate under the ocean floor was released into the water. This could happen during massive underwater landslides or earthquakes. Remember that a small amount of hydrate makes a huge amount of gas. The bubble of gas would rush towards the surface, expanding as it did.

If a huge bubble rose up under a ship, it would produce a massive hole in the sea underneath it. The ship would drop into the hole and sink instantly, settle to the sea bed and be covered in sediment thrown up by the escaping gas.

The methane gas would also cause problems for aircraft above the water. Methane is lighter than air, so it would rise upwards after leaving the water. An aircraft flying through the area would suffer engine failure or even ignite the gas. There is also evidence that a huge rush of gas would create a strong **magnetic field** which would affect compasses.

*This diagram shows what could happen to a ship if a huge bubble rose underneath it.*

Melting gas hydrate causes methane bubble on sea bed

Bubble rises to surface

Bubble causes 'hole' in surface of water into which ship falls

Ship fills with water and sinks

23

# True or false?

There are no reports of disappearances being faked in the Bermuda Triangle, but there are many cases of the truth about disappearances being ignored. Most of the books about the Bermuda Triangle discuss many cases of ships and aircraft which have disappeared or been found abandoned. The problem is that the facts of the cases are misquoted, fiddled with or simply ignored in order to make the cases seem more mysterious than they really are. Here are some of the cases. They are outlined in more detail on pages 10 and 11.

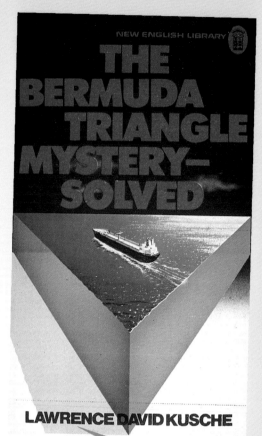

LAWRENCE DAVID KUSCHE

*Lawrence David Kusche investigated the facts behind dozens of Bermuda Triangle 'mysteries' and found that most had a simple answer.*

## Flight 19

(five bombers and a rescue plane, vanished in 1945) There are reports that the flight leader sent a message saying 'This is an emergency. We seem to be off course. We cannot see land ... repeat ... we cannot see land' and 'We don't know which way is west. Everything is wrong ... strange. We are not sure of any direction. The ocean doesn't look as it should.' These reports are not true. The flight leader was very new to the area and it's likely that he led the flight out to sea instead of back to land. Also, the Martin Mariner rescue plane did not simply disappear. A ship at sea saw an aeroplane explode at the same time as it disappeared from **radar** screens. The weather **deteriorated** badly, making the search almost impossible, otherwise wreckage may have been found.

## Star Tiger

(airliner, vanished in 1948)
Contrary to the stories of the captain reporting good flying conditions, the weather was not good – there were strong head winds and heavy cloud cover, which made navigation difficult. The aircraft may also have run out of fuel because the strong head winds would have made the journey take longer than expected.

# DC-3

(airliner, vanished in 1948)
There are false reports that the pilot said he could 'see the lights of Miami', but it is likely that he was lost and over deep ocean. The DC-3 is known to have had a faulty radio, so it could not have made an emergency call.

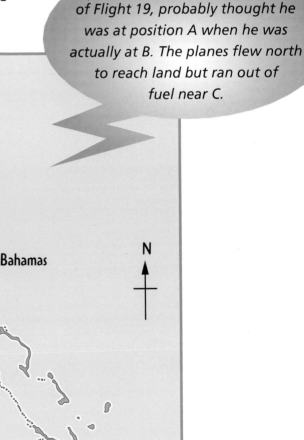

*Lieutenant Taylor, leader of Flight 19, probably thought he was at position A when he was actually at B. The planes flew north to reach land but ran out of fuel near C.*

# Muddled reports

All of these are ships that, according to several writers, disappeared mysteriously in the Bermuda Triangle. Again, there is more to the stories than is often reported.

## Atalanta

The *Atalanta* was a training ship that disappeared in 1880 on a voyage which included a leg through the Triangle. What reports do not mention is that nobody knows where the ship actually vanished. It also had a very inexperienced crew and would have encountered bad weather in the area it was sailing through.

## Rubicon

In October 1944, this 90-tonne Cuban cargo ship was found drifting and abandoned off Florida with only a dog on board. The crew had mysteriously vanished. Or had they? Reports from the time say it was in port in Havana, Cuba when the **moorings** broke in a **hurricane** and the ship drifted away, leaving the crew stranded ashore.

## Bella

This British ship was sailing from Rio de Janeiro to Jamaica in 1854 when it vanished 'without trace'. It was probably overloaded and may have capsized. Wreckage was found six days after it left Rio, when it would have been nowhere near the Triangle.

## Freya

The German **barque** *Freya* was found with its crew gone and its masts broken after sailing from Cuba. Supposedly a victim of the Triangle, in fact, it sailed from Mexico and was found in the Pacific Ocean, not the Atlantic.

## Raifuku Maru

This Japanese freighter vanished in the Triangle in 1925 after sending the alarming radio message 'Danger like dagger now. Come quick!' This message may be made up, since there was radio interference, and the passenger liner *Homeric* actually saw the freighter sink with all the crew aboard in 'huge waves'.

## Why falsify stories?

People are more interested in the mysterious than the **mundane**, and books about the mysterious are often best-sellers. This is certainly true of the Bermuda Triangle mystery. Several writers have written books on the subject which build up the mystery by telling only half the story.

Most famous of Bermuda Triangle authors is Charles Berlitz, who wrote two books in the 1970s. The first, *The Bermuda Triangle*, sold 20 million copies in 30 languages and made Berlitz a rich man. It led to television programmes, newspaper articles and more books, and massive hype about what may not be a mystery at all.

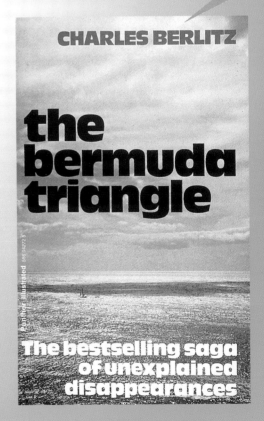

*The cover of Charles Berlitz's best-selling book of 'unexplained' mysteries.*

CHARLES BERLITZ

the bermuda triangle

The bestselling saga of unexplained disappearances

# In conclusion

Of all the world's mysteries, that of the Bermuda Triangle seems to be supported by the weakest evidence. On one side of the argument are writers who claim that something supernatural is going on. They ignore scientific evidence of fierce storms, **magnetic anomalies** and strong **currents**. On the other side are people, not necessarily scientists, who claim that there is no mystery at all, but that disappearances have natural causes and are no more frequent than probability would suggest. These include the United States government, Coast Guard and Navy.

*A picture-postcard scene on the coast of Bermuda. Nothing strange in sight!*

There is no doubt that there are a few cases which are a true mystery, where a ship, boat or plane was definitely inside the Bermuda Triangle and really disappeared without trace.

When so many of the disappearances of ships, aircraft and people which are claimed to be mysterious have plausible natural explanations, you could conclude that the biggest mystery is how the Bermuda Triangle mystery ever started!

# Make up your own mind

Now you have read about the Bermuda Triangle and the possible explanations for the disappearances there, can you draw any conclusions? Do you feel that you can dismiss any of the theories without investigating them further? Do you have any theories of your own?

What about the UFO theory, or the time-slip theory? Can you rule either one out? Perhaps one is the answer, and it depends on scientific principles that we don't understand yet. While it might be strange that no trace of a ship or aircraft is found, can this be taken as proof that something strange is going on? Do you think that bad weather and human error are more likely explanations? And what about the **methane** hydrate theory? Could this be the answer?

*Mysteries make good reading, as this article from the* People *newspaper in 1991 demonstrates. It simply retells Triangle stories.*

Try to keep an open mind. Bear in mind that if scientists throughout history had not bothered to investigate everything that appeared to be strange or mysterious, many scientific discoveries may never have been made.

# Fateful flight of the Avengers

## AIRMEN VANISH WITHOUT TRACE

**EVER since the first seamen set sail, the vast oceans have been sources of myth and mystery.**

Best documented of these was last century's riddle of the Mary Celeste, the ship which was found eerily abandoned in the Atlantic, east of the Azores.

Her sails were tattered and below deck there was chilling evidence which suggested hurried flight – yet the ship's log remained intact and its last entry, made nine days before, gave no hint of impending trouble.

The mystery remained unsolved even after a British Vice Admiralty court of inquiry, as it does today.

*Far more recently, voyagers of the sea and of the air have come to fear the Bermuda Triangle, a vaguely defined area somewhere east of Bermuda.*

One student of the unexplained, Ivan Sanderson, has theorised that the mysterious triangle is one of a dozen areas called "vile vortices" – another infamous vortex is the so-called Devil's Sea off the coast of Japan – where baffling forces are said to cause ships to vanish.

One of the earliest of these fateful missions in the Bermuda Triangle began on December 5, 1945, when five US Avenger torpedo bombers

roared off the runway of the Fort Lauderdale Naval Air Station in Florida.

Flight Instructor Lieutenant Charles G Taylor was leading 13 crewmen of Flight 19 on a routine navigational training exercise. Their course lay over an area bounded by Bermuda, Florida and Puerto Rico – the area which is now recognised as the Bermuda Triangle.

Flight 19 began smoothly enough but at 3.40pm an unsettling message from Taylor to another plane in the squadron was picked up by Lieutenant Robert Cox who was at that moment airborne over Fort Lauderdale on another exercise.

"What is your trouble?" Cox asked Taylor.

"Both my compasses are out and I am trying to find Fort Lauderdale," Taylor replied.

For 45 minutes Cox tried to ascertain Taylor's position and to direct him to land by orienting him towards the sun. But although it was a clear day, Taylor seemed unable to find it.

Finally, Taylor's transmission faded until it stopped. Then, inexplicably radio went dead, too, and he returned to the field at Fort Lauderdale. The ground station at Port Everglades

ever, had established intermittent contact with the troubled Flight 19, confirming Cox's observations. Finally, at about 5.15pm the ground station heard a forlorn message from Flight 19:

"We'll fly west until we hit the beach or run out of gas."

The authorities at Fort Lauderdale ordered a search but the Mariner was not heard of again.

For the next five days, search planes flew more than 930 sorties over the area, but not a scrap of wreckage from either the Avengers or the Mariner was ever recovered.

Most analysts blame these and other disappearances in the area on normal hazards of the sea and air. But what happened still remains a profound mystery.

More recently, we have learned of an equally mysterious leap across space and time, which occurred within the triangle – 25 years after the flight of the Avengers, almost to the day.

There was a "strange cigar-shaped cloud," recalled Bruce Gernon Jr, which gave him the first hint that his flight on December 4, 1970, would be out of the ordinary.

Gernon had just taken off from his Beachcraft Bonanza from Andros Island in the Bahamas, bound for Palm Beach, Florida.

He remembers accelerating quickly to avoid the thick cloud, but it seemed to rise to meet him.

The plane seemed to pick up unnatural speed, and for several seconds Gernon and his father experienced weightlessness. Then the aeroplane entered a green-ish-white haze – not the blue sky he had seen ahead.

*Through the haze he spotted a stretch of land and, calculating his flight time, took it to be the Bimini Keys, an island east of Miami. Minutes later, Gernon recognised it as Miami beach itself.*

Landing at Palm Beach, Gernon checked his clock. A trip that normally took him about 75 minutes had taken him only 45. And he had burned 12 fewer gallons of fuel than usual.

To this day, Gernon considers himself a lucky voyager in the Bermuda Triangle, having lived to tell of the inexplicable time warp.

# Glossary

**barque** a type of sailing cargo-ship with three masts, popular in the late 19th century

**black hole** a region of space where the gravity is so strong that not even light can escape from it

**collier** a medium-sized cargo-ship designed to carry bulk cargoes such as coal

**condenses** turns from gas to liquid because of cooling

**continental shelf** the edge of a continent, where the depth of the ocean increases dramatically. The continental shelf can be hundreds of kilometres from the continent's coastline.

**current** a flow from one place to another

**decompose** to break down complex chemicals into more simple chemicals. The chemicals in animals and plants decompose when the animals and plants die.

**deteriorate** get worse

**electrical storm** a storm in which there is lightning and thunder

**electric current** the flow of electrical charge from one place to another. It is normally the flow of tiny particles called electrons.

**freak wave** a wave considerably larger than the normal waves on the water at a given time. Freak waves are caused by smaller waves building up together.

**geographic pole** one of the two points (the North Geographic Pole and South Geographic Pole) where the axis around which the Earth revolves meets the Earth's surface

**hull** the main part of a boat or ship, which keeps the boat or ship watertight and forms its structure

**hurricane** an intense weather system which creates torrential rain and winds of more than 150 kilometres per hour. Hurricanes are called cyclones in the southern hemisphere.

**insurance** money paid to a person if his or her property is damaged, lost or stolen

**lightship** a permanently anchored ship carrying a beacon to guide other ships

**magma** hot, molten rock under the ground

**magnetic anomaly** a place on the Earth's surface where the Earth's magnetic field is distorted

**magnetic field** the area around a magnet where its magnetic force is felt. The Earth has a magnetic field shaped as though there was a bar magnet in its centre.

**magnetic pole** one of the two places on the surface of the Earth (called the North Magnetic Pole and the South Magnetic Pole) where the Earth's magnetic field is strongest

**methane** a naturally occurring gas often found under the ground with oil. Domestic gas supplies are methane.

**moorings** buoys or jetties where boats and ships are tied up

**mundane** another word for ordinary

**navigational** to do with navigation, which is planning and following a route at sea or in the air

**phenomenon** a remarkable or unexplained happening

**plankton** the numerous microscopic animals and plants that live in sea and fresh water

**radar** a device that uses radio waves to detect the position of ships, aircraft or coastlines

**rudder** a device at the stern (rear) of a boat, ship or aircraft which is used to make it turn from side to side

**sabotage** deliberately making things go wrong

**salvage tug** a large tug used for towing ships or oil rigs, or for salvaging ships after accidents

**schooner** a traditional type of sailing-ship with two or more masts

**sediment** mud, silt, sand or small pieces of rock which are carried along by a river before settling to the bottom when the river slows down near the sea

**sloop** a small sailing-ship

**structural failure** failure of the actual structure of a ship or plane, such as a hull which breaks in two or a wing that snaps off

**tornado** a swirling mass of air which reaches down from a storm cloud to the ground, normally up to 100 metres across, in which there are winds of more than 300 kilometres per hour

**vortex** a fast-spinning swirl of air or water

# Index